Honest, Honey, That's How It Happened

Humorous and Heartwarming Stories and Insight into Marriage

Russ Towne

Russ Towne Publishing
Campbell, CA
www.RussTowne.com
RussTowne@yahoo.com

Editing: Shayla Eaton, CuriouserEditing.com
Cover Design: Joleene Naylor
Interior Layout: Gail Nelson, e-book-design.com
Cover image courtesy of Yelet and Canstockphoto

ISBN 978-0-692804-23-0

Printed in the United States of America

Also Written By Russ Towne

Nonfiction

Reflections from the Heart of a Grateful Man

From the Heart of a Grateful Man

Reflections of a Grateful Man

Slices of Life—An anthology
of the selected nonfiction stories of several writers

Stop Peeing in the Kitty Litter

Fiction

Touched—Short stories and flash fiction

Palpable Imaginings—An anthology of fictional short stories
by several writers in various genres.

Poetry

Kaleidoscope

Tickletoe Tree Poetry—Humorous rhyming story poems for
children and those who are young at heart

Heart Whispers—An anthology of the selected works
of over twenty poets

Books for Young Children

The Beach That Love Built

Tickletoe Tree Poetry

A Day in the Shade of a Tickletoe Tree

The Grumpadinkles

Zach and the Toad Who Rode a Bull

Misty Zebracorn

V. G. and Dexter Dufflebee

Ki-Gra's REALLY, REALLY BIG Day!

The Duck Who Flew Upside Down

Clyde and Friends

Clyde and Hoozy Whatzadingle

Clyde and I Help a Hippo to Fly

Rusty Bear and Thomas Too

Clyde and I

Blogs

A Grateful Man (nonfiction uplifting posts): RussTowne.com

A Grateful Man's Poetry: AGratefulMansPoetry.com

Imaginings of a Grateful Man (fictional short stories):
ImaginingsofaGratefulMan.com

Clyde and Friends (about writing children's stories):
ClydeandFriends.com

Acknowledgments

Thank you to My Beloved for so generously participating in many of the experiences that I've attempted to faithfully capture in these stories.

Thank you also to the publishing professionals whose work enhanced this book.

Shayla Eaton of Curiouser Editing for copyediting.

Joleene Naylor for cover design.

Gail Nelson for book design.

Dedicated to My Beloved for all the reasons mentioned in this book, and many, many more.

I love you.

Contents

"We're all a little weird, and life's a little weird. And when we find someone whose weirdness is compatible with ours we join up with them and fall in mutual weirdness and call it love."
—Dr. Seuss

Introduction

My Beloved and I were married in 1979, and perhaps remarkably, despite many ups, downs, and all-arounds, we still love each other after all these years.

I've heard it said that the best relationships help smooth the rough edges of those in them. That has proven to be the case with My Beloved and me. At ages twenty-one and twenty, respectively, we both came into the relationship with a *lot* of rough edges.

We were like rough stones thrown together into the rock tumbler of life. She and I went round and round, noisily banging into each other, but we slowly ground each other's rough edges down, and were always there with, and for, each other.

Our relationship hasn't always been fun, and was often quite noisy, but over time, we both grew more polished, shined more brightly, and became a lot better for the experience.

We learned that life can often be rocky and it pays to keep rolling. That's the stone-cold truth that we never take for *granite*. (Hopefully, these are the last of the puns you'll have to suffer through in this book.)

We learned, and are still learning, much about our relationship, each other, and ourselves along the way, and have become better people as we've worked together to build a stronger relationship. We're happy with, and proud of, what we've created.

It is my hope that readers who are considering marriage for the first time, are taking another stab at it at some point in the future, or those who are already in one may take away something of value from reading *Honest, Honey, That's How It Happened.*

May these stories touch your heart and tickle bone. We've enjoyed living many of them, and are grateful to have survived the rest of them.

Too Stubborn and Selfish

Some folks thought we'd never make it as a couple. Here is the story of one of them.

A religious leader we'd asked to be the official at our wedding ceremony agreed to do so if we'd take a compatibility questionnaire. He gave it to all couples he officiated for. We weren't fond of the idea but knew the man was kind and if he thought it was a good idea and the information might be useful to us, then it probably would be.

So we each filled out a lengthy questionnaire and gave it to him. When the results came back, he ushered us into his office, sat us down, and in a solemn voice said something to the effect that based on our answers to the survey, we were both very stubborn and selfish; so stubborn and selfish, in fact, that the odds of us remaining married to each other were probably very small.

He seemed to be diplomatically attempting to talk us out of marrying each other, or trying to at least have us seriously consider whether we were ready for marriage, especially marriage to each other.

We agreed that we were both stubborn and selfish and acknowledged how that could be a huge challenge to a happy marriage, but we were in love and wanted to get married anyway.

We went ahead with our wedding, for we knew something he didn't:

We were both too stubborn to give up on each other, and too selfish to let the love we had for each other slip away.

Beautifully Imperfect

When My Beloved and I selected wedding and engagement rings for her, we intentionally selected two stones, a diamond and ruby (the latter being her birthstone) that had two small imperfections in them. The beautiful but imperfect gems were there to remind us that two imperfect people were joining together to create something beautiful.

My Beloved's cooking was so good (and my willpower so weak) that within six months of our wedding, I'd gained so much weight that my ring needed to be resized.

My Beloved took it to the jewelers and when she returned it to me, she'd had them add a diamond and ruby, each with minor imperfections in them.

Her Hippie Husband

I'd been so wrapped up in getting everything ready for our wedding that it wasn't until some time after 6:00 p.m. on a Saturday night—the night before our wedding—that I remembered that I hadn't gotten a haircut. My hair was longer than it had ever been.

Due to my four years of military science classes in high school, my hair had been cut quite at a time when nearly all the boys in school had long hair, so when I got out of high school, I'd let it grow and grow, with the intention of getting it cut before my wedding.

I drove all over town looking for an open barbershop that Saturday night in October of 1979, and failed.

There I was standing at the end of the aisle with hair that looked like a cross between something out of a disco movie and what you'd often see on a man in a VW bus with psychedelic paint all over it.

I can just imagine what My Beloved's relatives must have thought as they saw her walking down the aisle toward me.

There were probably some badly bitten tongues that day!

9

Not Off to a Great Start

We were so exhausted by our wedding preparations, the ceremony, and reception afterward, that about thirty minutes after we drove off to start our honeymoon, we missed a turn. Not just any turn. It was a six-lane freeway with lots of highly visible signs that practically shouted, "TURN HERE, YOU IDIOT!"

Worse, we didn't notice we missed the turn for about an hour! By the time we realized our mistake and backtracked, our eyes were blurring and we knew we could go no farther that night.

We stopped at the nearest motel we could find. It was cheap and near the entrance of the correct freeway. It was also apparently a place where many couples went to for liaisons, because the manager took one look and refused to book a room to us, assuming we were just two young lovers using her hotel for a quick fling. This is despite the fact that we both wore wedding rings. (I guess she'd seen that ploy before.)

I was in no mood to have to deal with the manager's efforts to attempt to protect my bride's virtue from me.

I became indignant and angry, and then told the manager that the marriage certificate was in our car and I'd go get it. She finally relented, and we got a room.

To Gnome Me Is to Love Me

When My Beloved and I went on our honeymoon, we were young and on a very tight budget. We drove to various places. During the trip, we took a detour to the Oregon Caves. On our way to them, on a little two-lane road, we drove by a home whose yard was absolutely covered in gnomes. Intrigued, we turned around and went back to look at the Gnome Home.

It turned out that is exactly what the homeowners hoped drivers would do, as they sold gnomes. The inside of their home/ store was covered in gnomes too. Perhaps it was due to the magic of being on our honeymoon, or perhaps it was the magic of the gnomes themselves, but whatever the reason, Gnomes have always had a special place in our hearts and homes, and they are always welcome.

Due to our financial situation at the time, we left that little store with only a little round pin and a calendar, but both had special meaning to us—and still do. The pin says, "To gnome me is to love me," and depicts a young gnome couple sitting on the long neck of a goose as they fly off on their honeymoon. I've always loved the sight of flying geese, and we were on our honeymoon, so the illustration had even deeper meaning for us. And like that gnome couple, we've had help along the way. Ours came from the love and support of family and friends, and perhaps a little magic from our gnome friends.

Our marital flight has hit some downdrafts, other unexpected turbulence, and even some major storms over the years, but no matter what, we've always found a way to keep flying.

Clueless

Most people who know me probably think I'm a reasonably intelligent man. My Beloved knows better. Case in point:

My Beloved and I got married when we were in our early twenties, and right after our wedding ceremony, we received a copy of what I thought was just a cute little souvenir certificate (mistake #1) of the wedding signed by the person officiating the ceremony and our two witnesses.

In my haste to begin our honeymoon, I inadvertently laid heavy luggage on top of the marriage certificate (mistake #2).

As we began unpacking at our destination, My Beloved noticed the wrinkled and slightly torn marriage certificate and handed it to me. I should have paid better attention to the look on her face (mistake #3) and if I had had a functioning brain cell in my head, I might have found a way to salvage the situation. Instead, I made the situation far worse.

As My Beloved handed the mangled document to me, I figured it was too far gone to be saved (mistake #4) and that we could just buy another one from the state that would have equal sentimental value to My Beloved (mistake #5), so in front of her, I began to finish ripping it the rest of the way in two (mistakes #6, #7, #8, to infinity).

As I was in mid-rip, she screamed, "Stop! What are you

doing to our marriage certificate!?"

That's not quite how either of us had dreamed our honeymoon would start. If she had killed me right then, I doubt a jury would have convicted her.

To her credit, she didn't end the marriage right then and there. Or maybe it just proves she isn't quite as bright as people think she is!

Whatever the reason, I'm eternally grateful that she has hung in there with me for all these years. It hasn't always been easy, but it has rarely been boring.

And yes, we still have that original, mangled, nearly-four-decade-old marriage certificate with a tear halfway down it. It has gone through some tough times with us, but like our marriage, has always found the strength to stay together no matter what.

Bickering and Bounced Checks

When My Beloved and I had begun dating, I was self-employed in a business that sold seep watering systems (they were similar to drip systems and saved a lot of water versus conventional systems at the time).

By the time we were engaged, heavy rains had greatly reduced demand for my product, and by the time we were married, the year had been so rainy that I found myself heavily in debt. Through it all, My Beloved's faith in me never wavered, and she didn't back out of our engagement even when I was forced to close the business.

When we returned from our honeymoon, I was unemployed, heavily in debt, and my checkbook was running on fumes.

Being two stubborn and selfish young people, we foolishly bickered a lot on our honeymoon, so much so that I sometimes jokingly refer to that time as our "bickermoon."

Whatever it was called, we knew it was definitely over when we returned home to our small apartment to find three bounced checks. One of them was due to an error in my checkbook, and the other two due to our not-so-friendly neighborhood bank cashing the third and largest one I'd written first. That way, the bank ensured that the other two smaller that would have cleared also bounced and they could charge overdraft fees for all three.

Unfortunately, one of the smaller checks was to my mother-in-law. Not a great way to make a good early impression!

Scrambling to Get a Job

After the bounced checks, I of course immediately began to look for a job. I didn't have a college degree, and was unqualified for the better-paying jobs. Despite being an introvert, I took a job in sales, figuring I'd be able to quickly make more money that way. It was a draw-against-commission type of compensation in a technical recruiting agency in Silicon Valley.

I planned to only remain in a sales-type role until I could find something more suitable to my analytical personality. I worked hard at it and did well enough that it led to a nearly thirty-year sales-related career, initially in agencies, and then in-house at various high-tech companies. After years in recruiting management roles, I went off on my own for eighteen years, eventually owning high-tech recruiting-related firms.

Our first child came thirteen months after our wedding, and My Beloved (with my full support) decided to stay at home to be a full-time mom. Despite all the challenges I faced in a hyper-cyclical industry, I have no doubt My Beloved had the harder and more important role.

Being a one-income family at a time when most of our peers were both working full-time jobs came with hardships, but we've never regretted her choice.

The Day My Beloved Got Me Fired

Speaking of that first job, there came a day when I had to take time off from work due to the simultaneous removal of all of my wisdom teeth. I'd gotten my boss's approval for the time off in advance. Unfortunately and unbeknownst to me, at about the time that I was sitting in the oral surgeon's chair, an ugly stomach flu was gaining strength inside me.

When I returned home, I was in pain and groggy from the surgery, anesthesia, and stitches. I'd planned to rest in bed for the rest of that day and then go back to work the next morning. It didn't quite work out that way.

I hadn't even made it to the bed when the symptoms of the flu hit me full force. I'll spare you the gory details, but it is probably sufficient to say that I was one very sick and miserable young man. I couldn't sleep and became very weak from making many trips between our bathroom and bed.

My Beloved called in sick for me the next morning. When I'd begun working at that firm, I'd heard from other employees that my boss (the owner) had the habit of calling to check to see if his employees were actually sick at home or going out on job interviews, but I'd never been sick as his employee so I didn't think much of it, at least not until the morning My Beloved called in sick for me and explained the situation to my boss.

Shortly afterward, my boss telephoned and asked My Beloved to have me come to the phone. We didn't have a cordless phone in those days, and our only phone was about as far away from our bed as it could be in our modest apartment, so against her better judgment, My Beloved relayed his request to me. I badly needed that job and thought that perhaps he needed to ask me for some important information, so I crawled out of bed and barely made it to the phone. Once he was assured that I was at home and wasn't at an interview, he abruptly ended the call, and then I dragged myself back to bed.

About an hour later, the phone rang again, and the process was repeated.

Unbelievably, a short time later, my boss called a third time. By now, I couldn't even get out of bed and was too weak to speak in any case.

My Beloved had had enough. She told him politely but firmly that I was too ill to come to the phone.

He shouted, "Look, little lady, I want you to get Russ on the phone right now!" That did it. My Beloved hardly ever swears. In fact, until then, I don't think that I'd ever heard her say an expletive that would have raised eyebrows in a holy place, but apparently, she had saved up the granddaddy of all swear words for just a moment as this.

The word exploded from her mouth into the phone, followed quickly by the word "YOU!" and then she hung up.

She came to tell me what she'd done, but I'd already heard her. My Beloved was concerned that she'd gotten me fired and knew how badly we needed the income. I wanted to congratulate her for standing up to the man, but was so ill that all I could muster was a slight grin. Hopefully, she saw the twinkle in my eyes that went with it. I was—and remain—very proud of My Beloved for not letting him bully her.

After he recovered a bit from the shock, he dialed our number again. She let the phone ring. Five rings. Ten. Twenty rings. Finally, she picked up the receiver and immediately placed it back on the hook. The phone rang again. She let it ring several times, and then picked up the receiver, set it on a table, and walked away.

He never did get to tell her off.

Of course, I was fired as soon as I was well enough to return to the office, but that just saved me the hassle of quitting. When I recovered from my illness, I went in to the office to collect my belongings, but he'd hidden my family photos and a few other personal items in his office. I had to threaten to call the police and report the theft before he quickly returned them. I've never been happier to leave a job than I was that day, and I learned an important lesson:

My Beloved can stand up for herself—and it's not wise to make her angry!

Honest, Honey, That's How It Happened

WAY Too Much of a Good Thing

I weighed 148 pounds and stood an inch shy of six feet tall on our wedding day. I wasn't merely skinny—I was gaunt, despite gobbling up huge amounts of nutritionally horrible and calorie-laden junk food virtually every meal of every day. No matter what I ate or how many calories it contained, I never gained even one measly much-needed pound. Not even an ounce.

Then I got married. To say that marriage brings on many changes is about as much of an understatement as saying that having a baby might involve an occasional loss of sleep or a slight lifestyle change.

My Beloved cooked healthy and tasty meals. That was wonderful! A smart man would have just stuck with those meals. I, naturally, took a different approach. I ate all those good meals and augmented them with the junk food I'd become addicted to. That combination caused me to gain weight. Yay! I gained twenty-five pounds and for the first time in my life, I felt good about how much I weighed and felt I finally looked normal. My new weight—173 pounds—was perfect. I was ecstatic!

My euphoria lasted about thirty seconds as I blew right on by perfection, past pudgy, and solidly into "Oh my god, how in the world did I get here?" territory.

I gained forty-eight pounds in six months. I added weight

so fast that I ended up with stretch marks that I still have nearly four decades later.

I've been fighting the battle of the bulge ever since, though as I've gotten older (and hopefully at least somewhat wiser), my eating habits have somewhat improved.

So, this is a cautionary tale. If you are young, and eat a *lot* of junk food, and if you have the chance to marry someone who is a good cook, be sure to think through *all* the ramifications first!

To Protect His Heart

My Beloved was once asked in front of a group of fifty or sixty men, "What do you believe is your most important job as a wife?" Some of the men looked at me to see if I knew what her answer would be. I just shrugged, as I had no idea.

She replied, "To protect his heart."

She added, "It's my most important job to never break his heart."

I cherish that woman.

Water Fight!

Some of my favorite moments in life have occurred on a whim. For example, water fights between My Beloved and me. In the bathroom. They would often start innocently enough, such as when I'm in the shower and she turns on hot water full blast in the bathroom sink, dropping the temperature of the water that's pouring on my shampoo-filled head to several degrees below freezing.

(Okay, I know that the water wasn't frozen yet and was probably slightly above freezing, but it *felt* like it was below freezing! And maybe she hadn't turned the hot water on quite full blast, but to this day, I contend that was only so she could claim to be innocent, while to me it looked like pretty damning evidence of premeditated malice.)

I let out an indignant bellow that could probably be heard by neighbors several blocks away, as shampoo got into my eyes and mouth.

And did I hear an apology from My Beloved? *No.* Just a little giggle. Then another, slightly louder (and to my water-clogged ears, sounding a bit more taunting.)

Well, two can play at that game, so I raised the shower head over the top of the shower wall and aimed the spray right at her, drenching her clothes, hair, and everything else. Now it was her turn to shriek indignantly. And, oh, how she shrieked! You'd think I was killing her! I was afraid the neighbors would hear and think something nefarious was going on in our home, but I shouldn't have worried, because by then, they probably knew that some type of craziness was always going on in our house.

Being the mature woman and mother that she was, and knowing that our three impressionable young children were no doubt by now clustered on the other side of the bathroom door wondering if their parents had gone insane, she naturally and sensibly called a truce, right?

Yeah, right. She waited until I went back to rinsing the shampoo off my head, and out of my eyes and mouth, and then grabbed a large glass—it must have held at least two or three gallons (well, that's my side of the story and I'm sticking to it)—and filled it with ice-cold water, opened the shower door, and splashed it all over me.

Then the water fight began in earnest with howls of laughter, and water drenching everything from floor to ceiling, and all things in between.

When we were both half-drowned and had had enough, we negotiated a truce, which takes no small amount of mutual trust in such situations as we stared each other down—me with an itchy trigger finger on the shower head, and my steely-eyed foe holding two full water glasses primed for throwing.

We were both dripping from head to toe, and panting through aching jaws from laughing so hard.

We surveyed the damage we'd inflicted on our poor,

innocent bathroom, gave each other a knowing look, grabbed a bunch of dry towels from the closet, and began cleaning up the mess.

Such craziness is a large part of what brings the joy to us in our JOYoUS life.

We've learned that a good way to measure how happy a relationhip is, is to see how much zaniness and laughter occurs in it.

Honest, Honey, That's How It Happened

The experience I'm about to share may have been the most embarrassing day of my life—and considering how many such moments I've had, that is really saying something.

Many years ago, I'd volunteered to take a car load of stuff that my employer needed for the booth of a job fair to our area's convention center. When I arrived, I noticed with frustration that the road leading to the loading dock was long and narrow, and that there was an even longer queue of drivers waiting to unload their vehicles one by one as each eventually became the first in line at the single unloading point.

When I saw the line, I looked at my watch and sighed. Based on how slowly the line was moving, I estimated that if I were lucky, I'd probably just barely be able to unload, park my car, and get the booth set up in time for the stampede of thousands of job applicants waiting outside the front doors for the event to begin.

Finally, as my car reached the unloading area, I saw a fellow employee on the dock signaling that if I carried the stuff from my car to him, he'd relay it to the place where the booth was to be set up. Good plan!

Because it would not take long to unload the car and we were almost out of time—and in consideration of those waiting in line behind me—I left my car's engine running as I jumped out to begin unloading.

Out of habit, and in my haste, I locked the door as I got out. When I went to open a rear door, it wouldn't budge. Then it hit me. I'd locked my keys in my car with the engine running in front of a lot of people who counted on me to quickly unload and get out of their way.

I didn't quite panic yet. Thinking quickly, I began to check all the doors. Maybe I'd be lucky and one would be unlocked. Nope. My heart sank as I knew right then that it was going to be *that* kind of day.

I silently screamed to myself as I sized up the potential disaster I'd just created not only for myself and my company but for everyone around me.

My adrenaline surged as I tried to figure out how I was going to get out of this mess.

I looked for a spare key in the off chance My Beloved had put one under the car and that I might have forgotten it was there.

My luck was holding. No spare key.

By now, I was getting desperate and the glares of the people around me went from impatience to feelings that I'd prefer not to mention or even think about in mixed company (but if looks could kill, I'd have used up more lives than a dozen cats). I was in a bad situation that was rapidly deteriorating.

I came up with the idea to break the glass on my driver's side window, but I couldn't find anything to smash it with other than my fist or elbow. That glass suddenly looked thick and intimidating. I rationalized that I wouldn't be doing anyone any favors if I slashed an artery while shattering the window, what with all of the emergency vehicles they'd have to send. So, that not-so-brilliant idea was quickly scratched off my very short list of options.

I ran to the drivers of several cars who were queued up behind me and explained the situation. I don't recall their exact words at this wonderful news, but between their rolling eyes and comments muttered under their breath, I had a good idea that I'd just become their least favorite person on the planet. If tar and feathers or a rope had been handy, I think they'd have used them on me—and I wouldn't have blamed them.

Remember those scenes from the old westerns when the wagon train master yelled instructions and the information was shouted from one wagon to the next on down the line so that everyone would know what to do? That's about what it sounded like as I turned and raced back to my still-running car—except the tone of the modern-day drivers was a *lot* less friendly than the ones I remember in those movies.

I silently pleaded with my old car, "Please, *please* don't overheat."

People started to feverishly unload their cars and trudge the heavy equipment and boxes all along the line of vehicles as they tried to get their booths set up in time. They had to walk right by me. I apologized, but that didn't get the job done—theirs or mine.

Okay, one option left, and it was a long shot. I raced to a

phone and dialed my home phone number. I remembered that My Beloved had planned to run errands with our two young boys that morning, so I knew that she probably wouldn't be home to answer my call. As the phone rang, my brain screamed, *Be home, BE HOME!*

After several rings, My Beloved answered. The conversation went something like this:

Me: "Uh, honey, uh, could you drop everything and bundle the kids into your car and rush down to the back of the convention center with the spare key to my car, then park your car, and with the boys in tow, walk the spare keys over to me?"

My Beloved: (Silence.) "Why? Did you lose your keys?"

Me: I responded with my best "Who would do something silly like that?" tone in my voice: "No. I never lose my keys!" Then sheepishly added, "I locked my keys in the car . . ."

My Beloved: "Can you wait for a while? The convention center is forty minutes away and I'm right in the middle of—"

Me, interrupting her: "With the car running. At the loading dock. With a line of cars and a bunch of angry people stuck behind me."

My Beloved: "Oh." (More silence—but this time, I'm pretty sure I distinctly heard the sound of her eyes rolling.) "Okay. I'll be right down."

Have I mentioned lately how much I love that woman?

How NOT to Surprise My Beloved

I wanted to surprise My Beloved by buying a new car for her. I already knew the color, make, and model she wanted. I'd told her I was "out with a friend." I hadn't lied; the friend was with me—but I'd left out the little detail about wanting to surprise her with a new car.

The trouble was that the deal took a *lot* longer to transact than I'd anticipated. I called her a couple of times to keep postponing the time I'd arrive home. She was having a bad day and she got madder with each call. By the time I got home, it was *very* late, hours later than I'd originally planned, and she was steaming.

I came in acting sheepishly and told her, "Something happened to your car." (It had; it got replaced by a much better one, but she didn't know it yet.) At that point, my life expectancy was probably about two minutes.

I somehow convinced her to go outside. There she saw her brand-new car wrapped in a huge ribbon with a great big bow. A teddy bear and a bottle of champagne rested on the steering wheel.

It had been my turn to get a new car so she was greatly surprised when she got another new one before I got one. It pushed back my getting a new car for a long time but was well worth the delay to see her excitement and beaming smile.

Our day may have gone badly, but our evening ended well.

A Knock on the Door

I wanted to honor My Beloved and celebrate our twenty-fifth wedding anniversary in a special way. This is what I came up with (with a lot of help from my friends):

My wife heard a knock on the door and when she opened it, she was surprised to see me on one knee directly in front of her, with eleven men forming a semicircle behind me. We were each holding a long-stemmed red rose and began singing a rousing rendition of The Temptations song, "My Girl," to her. It even included some cool (or should I say, *groovy*) dance moves that the men had come up with and practiced at another location just prior to the knock on the door! We serenaded her, accompanied by a boom box playing the song.

Our audience grew as neighbors came out to see what was going on. They clapped and cheered us on.

When the song and dance were finished, each man in turn stepped forward and handed a long-stemmed red rose to My Beloved, gave her a hug and a kiss on the cheek, and congratulated her. I then gave a bouquet of twenty-five long-stemmed red roses—one for each year of our marriage—to her along with a big hug and kiss.

The kindness and thoughtfulness of the men helped to create a truly magical and memorable evening. While I'd known some of the men for years, I'd only recently met some of the others. They had driven up to two hours in heavy commute traffic to be there for the relatively brief experience. They all had other things that they could have been doing. Some had families waiting for them at their homes for dinner. Others took time off from work. They weren't professional singers or performers—just regular men who gave a special gift to a special woman and me.

My Beloved loved it, and so did I. It was a low-cost yet unforgettable way to commemorate and celebrate our major milestone.

The men had fun too.

Mission Improbable

My biological father was an avid golfer. He always dreamed of playing the Pebble Beach Golf Course. He and another man wanted to play the course together, so they began to pool their savings in a big five-gallon bottle kept at the other man's house. When the bottle was full and they could afford to go, his "friend" took all the money and spent it.

My biological father, who lived on the East Coast, was heartbroken knowing he'd never fulfilled his dream.

When he died, his wife told me that his last request was that I would scatter his ashes on the Pebble Beach Golf Course.

GULP! I tend to be a rule-follower, and if I don't like someone else's rules, I tend to change games—which is one reason I'm self-employed (my game, my rules)—but this request definitely fit into the rule-breaker side of things. I figured that if I fulfilled his last request, I would certainly be breaking many rules and most likely several laws.

I was torn. Badly.

Ultimately, blood proved thicker than mere rules and laws (and I have probably never in my life used the word *mere* in front of either of the words rules and laws).

I discussed my dilemma with My Beloved. She was no happier or comfortable with the request than I, and probably much less so, but she offered to come along to offer moral support. We both knew there was a chance I would be caught and arrested, and if she was with me, she could suffer a similar fate. She wanted to come anyway, and woe be to the person who tries to tell her no when she sets her mind to something.

When the day came, we drove to Pebble Beach, becoming more anxious with each mile, too nervous to enjoy the fantastic views on the way there.

We noted with growing concern that security vehicles and guards seemed to be everywhere. They had their own private army.

We scoped the perimeter like a couple on a secret mission. Actually, we *were* a couple on a secret mission. Piercing the perimeter looked like a really *bad* idea.

Our nerves were on edge, but we also noticed that along with the risk and danger, an element of excitement and adventure began to creep in.

The theme song from the original *Mission Impossible* TV show kept running through my head. Seriously.

My Beloved put the clay urn full of ashes in her purse as we parked our car. We walked through the magnificent clubhouse with its main room that is so large it has two huge and very impressive fireplaces.

The view was magnificent! We walked out the back of the clubhouse, across a patio filled with diners, down some steps, and onto a large lawn area that led out to a stone edge, which marked the end of the lawn and the beginning of a small beach several feet below, and the Monterey Bay.

The golf course's 18th hole was to our left, near the stone edge with the sudden drop-off in front of us. I don't recall what separated the course from the lawn near the stone edge, but it wasn't much of an obstacle. Perhaps a rope.

We had much bigger obstacles to deal with. First, parties of golfers were very often either on the green making their final putts, or walking to it. I couldn't just waltz onto the green and start spreading ashes all over it.

But the biggest obstacle was that a burly security guard must have decided we looked suspicious and began following us onto the long, beautiful green lawn that gently sloped down toward the bay.

Our hearts raced as we looked at each other, wondering what to do. We'd come too far to turn back now. In a whisper, I suggested that we sit on the edge of the lawn at the corner of the rock ledge, near the 18th hole, and try to look like sightseers.

The security guard hung back and off to our right about twenty feet away and appeared to be cleaning his nails. Yeah, right!

I decided to lay down parallel to the golf course and up against it with my back facing the guard. My Beloved took out her camera and pretended to take pictures, gradually moving her body into a position that would perfectly obstruct the guard's view as she reached into her purse and handed the urn to me without it being seen by the guard. I placed the clay container in front of me and covered it with a jacket.

There was no way I was going to be able to walk onto the green without immediately drawing attention to myself, being stopped, and possibly arrested.

We did catch a lucky break in that a strong wind was blowing inland from the bay. If I could time the space between the golf parties just right, and if I could throw the ashes into the wind without being seen by golfers on the course, people in the clubhouse, diners on the patio, and the ever-present and attentive guard, the ashes would float onto the 18th green. There were too many ifs for my taste, but it was the hand we'd been dealt so we'd try to play it.

The whole urn and ashes thing had kind of creeped me out, so I hadn't opened the lid of the urn since it had been handed to me on the East Coast.

That proved to be a big mistake! When I think of ashes, I think of those soft, floaty things that gently rise from a campfire, so when I reached into the urn, I expected to feel kind of a soft, light powder.

My eyes must have gotten huge when what I felt bore no semblance to anything even remotely resembling ashes! It felt like a nearly solid mass with a consistency not unlike sandstone. (It should be noted here that we tried to be as respectful as possible through the whole process, as I was aware that what I was touching was the last physical remains of the man who was one of two humans responsible for bringing me into this world, and that his remains should be treated with respect.)

Still, I was freaked out. It might have even been funny under other circumstances, but at the moment, laughter was about the furthest thing from my mind as I felt a surge of panic.

I groaned, and then whispered the latest problem to My Beloved. She gave a startled expression followed by a shrug and her, "Well, I guess you're just going to have to deal with it" look that I knew so well.

It was My Beloved who came up with the next tactic, whispering, "I'll distract the guard," as she picked up the camera and walked away.

I looked over my shoulder, following her with my eyes, and watched the guard with my peripheral vision as I feverishly began scraping the contents of the urn with my fingernails, trying to loosen it all.

I then waited for that hoped-for critical moment when everything aligned perfectly: the 18th green had no one on or near it, the guard was facing away, and the wind was gusting in from the bay. I just had to hope that no one else walked onto the lawn and that everyone was too far away to notice what I was up to.

The seconds turned to minutes, dragging on interminably, while I continued scraping the contents of the urn as My Beloved continued slowly walking to the other side of the lawn, pretending to take photos of the gorgeous scenery.

The guard had the choice of watching My Beloved to his right, turning his back on me, or vice versa. He chose her. Good choice!

Just then, the 18th green was clear, and I slowly and nonchalantly stretched my right arm high over onto the golf course as if I were stretching contentedly without a care in the world. As I did so, I opened my hand and flicked the contents with my fingers. To my great relief and with substantial help from the wind, they scattered over the 18th green. I did this several more times, never knowing if the next toss would end with my arrest, but lucking out every time.

I signaled to My Beloved when I was done, and we reversed the process, getting everything back into her purse.

As I stood up, I felt as though a huge weight had been lifted from my shoulders. Mission accomplished!

The two successful secret agents soaked in their success, and even took a victory lap of sorts. We walked into the clubhouse and sat in some beautiful chairs. I ordered my biological father's favorite drink, a dirty vodka martini on the rocks, and My Beloved ordered a glass of champagne.

We made a toast to him.

Then we toasted to what we'd accomplished together.

I don't recall ever having a drink I enjoyed more.

No Star in All the Heavens

The story of the star that sits atop our Christmas tree goes back nearly forty years. I was a young single man whose business was failing. Finances were very tight. I had enough money to buy a Christmas tree but not enough for ornaments or other decorations. A young woman I was dating at the time saw how bare the tree looked. She made a big star out of a piece of cardboard that she'd cut out herself and then wrapped it in aluminum foil she taped to it. It sure looked good on top of my nearly bare tree! A year later, that young woman became my wife.

That star has sat in the place of honor on all of our Christmas trees. During the good years, it reminds us of times when things weren't so good, and during rough years, it reminds us that bad times don't last forever. But most of all, it reminds us how blessed we are to have the love of our family and friends.

Over the years, the star became ragged-looking and has often been repaired by adding more aluminum foil and tape. My wife sometimes suggests that we replace it with a store-bought treetop ornament, but I can't bring myself to do it, because no star in all the heavens is more beautiful to me than the one that sits atop our tree.

Date Nights

My Beloved and I learned long ago that it was critical for the health of our marriage to have at least weekly Date Nights where just the two of us spend time together.

When we skip Date Nights, the gears of our relationship are much more likely to get out of sync and begin to grind. Little irritations can become big problems, and important things are more likely to go unsaid.

Carving out time for each other helps remind us that our relationship and our spouse are important to us.

We often set aside a specific evening of the week for Date Night, but sometimes our usual night isn't ideal for one of us, so we find another night that same week that works for both of us. The important thing for our relationship is that Date Night consistently occurs every week, rather than whether it occurs on the exact same night each week. Flexibility, commitment, and positive attitudes help to keep our Date Nights happening and our relationship strong.

Our Date Nights can be expensive and elaborate, but often are neither. While we've found that getting out of the house is important for our Date Nights, what we do on them is less important so long as we both have an interest in or are at least open to the activities.

Since we love to eat, having dinner together tends to be one of our favorite things to do. We'll also sometimes go for a drive, go to the beach, take a walk, go to the movies, or whatever else we come up with to do together.

While we call it Date Night, our dates can be any time of the day or week. When we've been on tight budgets, breakfasts, lunches, and picnics, can be less expensive alternatives.

We also like to have weekends together or even just a weekend day. While eating breakfast at a favorite little restaurant in the Santa Cruz Mountains one Saturday, my wife mentioned that she was exhausted from working full time and going back to college for more mandatory post-grad college courses. I suggested that we go to a nearby park so she could rest. She suggested I buy a book so I'd have something to read while she napped. We took a couple of blankets that we kept in the trunk of the car and spread them out on a beautiful green lawn near towering redwood trees and a beautiful historic covered bridge over a stream on a sunny day. My Beloved fell asleep to the distant sounds of children playing, while I lay next to her reading a good book, watching birds soar overhead and observing families enjoying the day.

We were there for about three hours, and it was one of our favorite times together.

Romance can be kept alive in many ways, and some of the best for us often involves life's simple joys and pleasures.

LAAF SHMILY!

My wife and I sometimes write notes or sign cards to each other that end with LAAF! and/or SHMILY! It's not because we have forgotten how to spell the words *laugh* or *smile*. *LAAF* and *SHMILY* are acronyms for "Love Always And Forever" and "See How Much I Love You." We sometimes use them as quick reminders that we are there for each other forevermore.

We sometimes leave notes with no other message but LAAF SHMILY where the other will find them. Such notes take very little time, and like so many of the most important things in life, are free.

Keeping Lists

Some lists make life better and some worse. I've found that grocery lists come in handy, but lists of a person's transgressions, failings, imperfections, and mistakes do not. I'm blessed to have a wife who knows that the latter type of list can be toxic to relationships. If she kept such a list about me, it would be long indeed.

I believe that there *is* a kind of list that enhances relationships and our attitude toward them: Blessings Lists. They are lists of the *positive* attributes and actions of people. They remind me as to the many great things people bring to my life. Such blessings are much more likely to be about the time they shared, a kindness they showed, things I enjoy about them, their positive attributes, or a fault or mistake of mine they forgot, forgave, or ignored.

The most important blessings to me almost never involve money or material things. They are far more precious because they are things money can't buy. Things like loyalty, love, trust, and true intimacy.

When My Beloved and I focus on creating Blessings Lists, we can't help but feel grateful for each other.

What I Must Have in My Marriage

There was a time when I hadn't really thought through the relatively few things I *must have* to be happy in my marriage. The whole thing was kind of fuzzy to me. If I were asked the question on back-to-back days, the answers and the list of things would probably vary substantially and I often confused wants with needs.

That led to frustration and unhappiness, not only for me but for My Beloved. If I didn't really know what I must have in our marriage, how could she know what I needed?

When I finally stopped to figure out what I must have, I was shocked to find out how hard it was for me to come up with a short and accurate list.

I learned that if an item on the list was really about the actions or inactions or attitudes of My Beloved, then it really wasn't a must-have for me. My must-have list needed to be independent of her.

Items such as "She shouldn't gossip, lie to me, cheat, drive badly" wouldn't qualify for my must-have list, but these would:

"I must be in a marriage in which I'm:

Loved

Trusted

Respected

Appreciated

and in which:

My physical needs are met.

Fidelity is a given.

Now that I truly know my must-haves and I have them all in my marriage, everything else shrinks in importance and I tend to be much happier, content, and fulfilled. I no longer really care what color paint we use, what flowers we plant, or how the furniture in most of the rooms is arranged.

A Man with a Treasure

I know a man who has a true treasure for a wife, yet too often chooses to focus on her relatively few faults instead of celebrating and being grateful for all the ways he is amazingly blessed to have her in his life. At those times, that man is one of the biggest fools I know.

Sadly, I'm that man.

A Blessing

It is a blessing to me that My Beloved is a teacher of children in special education and loves them. I'm sure on many occasions she's thought when she comes home to me, she is coming home to yet another special education kid.

She has patiently stayed with this slow-learner (my words, not hers) for nearly four decades. I can still truthfully say to her: "You make me want to be a better man" and even "You make my days better just by being in them."

The Last Words They'll Hear

Every member of my family says "I love you" every time we leave each other, at the end of every call, and it is the last thing My Beloved and I say to each other at night.

No matter how, when, or where we die, "I love you" will be the last words the others will have heard from us.

There is something very comforting to me in that.

That Was You?

My Beloved and I met while playing hide-and-seek in the dark. When I was a youngster, all of our relatives lived out of state, so my family celebrated holidays with another family who were close friends and were in a similar situation. We tended to go to their house for the holidays. They lived in a cul-de-sac (we grew up calling them *courts*).

After each holiday meal, all the kids on the block would go out to play on the well-lit, low-traffic street. There must have been twenty or thirty of us at times. Our favorite game after darkness fell was hide-and-seek. We'd use the streetlight as "home base" or "safe" or whatever it was called.

A few years later, on another holiday, at a house three doors down from our friends', lived a family with three girls. They had a basketball hoop. One day, the three sisters challenged my two brothers and me to a game of basketball. None of the Towne boys were particularly athletic—and in my case, that is putting it very kindly—but we were boys and we were taller than them (and the extra height and reach is a big advantage in basketball) so we accepted the challenge. What could go wrong?

Everything. Talk about a setup! Those short girls were very athletic and very good at basketball. We got our clocks cleaned. The game wasn't even close.

Fast-forward to high school. I'm an introvert and in those days lacked confidence with girls, especially if I had any romantic interest in them. But I was comfortable with girls who were just friends because they were "safe." I wasn't trying to get them to like me romantically so I wasn't at risk emotionally with them. I didn't have to worry about the dreaded R-word (rejection) and could just be my goofy self. I could even flirt with them a bit if they flirted with me first.

I had an upper locker and two fun and flirty girls shared a locker below mine so we used to flirt and talk to each other a lot. Their best friend was a gal who had multiple sisters and she and her sisters all looked alike to me. I didn't know how many of the sisters there were and wasn't sure of their names so I just said hi when I saw any of them. So the girl and her sisters were just in the background, and I never really took much notice of any of them.

About three years after graduating high school, I was at a party where I knew all the girls pretty well—all except one. The latter was sitting with a girl I knew quite well and wanted to dance with, so I politely interrupted their conversation and asked my friend for a dance. As she got up, I jokingly said to the one who was still sitting on the couch, "Don't worry. I'll bring her back shortly."

Well, I didn't. The girl and I ended up dancing for half an hour. When we were done, I remembered my joking promise to the other girl and saw she was still sitting on the couch. I went over to her and jokingly apologized for breaking my promise and hogging her friend. She was gracious about it. I sat on the couch next to her and we began to talk.

Within minutes, the strangest thing happened. We didn't talk about what people in their late teens tend to talk about. We started to talk about our dreams, and not just generic dreams, very specific ones. For example, we both wanted to have two biological children and then adopt more. And the babies we wanted to adopt were some of the ones that were considered the least likely to be adoptable:

Those in the US who were missing one or more limbs, who were blind or deaf, or had other similar challenges, or a baby from another country who was in a very bleak situation and would likely die or face terrible choices as they grew up.

It became immediately clear that we shared the same dreams; so much so, that we began to finish each other's sentences, as we knew what the other was going to say before we said it.

My heart sank. I was reeling. I remember thinking, *"Uh-oh, how many girls in the whole world could possibly share my exact dreams? Oh-no, I'm probably going to end up having to marry this girl and I don't even know her, and I don't even know whether I like her, let alone love her."* I was not at all sure this was a good thing, and was completely unprepared for this situation.

I ended up asking her out for coffee after the party. My car must have been in the shop because I had my dad's Travelall (picture a huge SUV-type monster with four-wheeling, off-road tires that were so big I could barely climb into it, and at 4' 11" she was a full foot shorter than me). Like most girls that age, in those days, she was wearing a short dress.

It became obvious that getting her into the vehicle was going to be kind of tricky. But she was game for it so I began to help lift/push/shove her upward. At a critical point when she was balanced precariously, I had no choice but to place my hands on her behind to finish helping her into the vehicle. But I did what was necessary to help her as any gentleman would do under the circumstances.

At the coffee shop, I remember that she had lemonade and I had hot cocoa and we shared an order of onion rings. (I don't recommend having any two of those items together, by the way. What were we thinking?)

We talked for a while and when it was time to take her home, I had to help her get back into my vehicle. Well, I can't say that it broke my heart. A man's gotta do what a man's gotta do.

She lived with her parents and as I turned onto her cul-de-sac, memories started flooding back to me. This was the same street I'd played on as a kid on holidays for so many years. When she pointed to her house, it was the one with the basketball hoop she and her sisters had used to massacre my brothers and me so many years before.

It became clear in an instant. I'd played hide-and-seek in the dark with her when we were young children, and she was the one who had been there with the flirty girls at the lockers!

She gave a knowing look to me and smiled as she could see it all falling into place in my head. She'd known all along.

She kidded me about the basketball game, and about how

I didn't seem to notice her at all through high school, even though she was best friends and always with the two girls who had the locker below mine.

She said she'd had a crush on me all through high school. My head began to swell, but I also began to feel bad about not noticing her sooner. Both feelings quickly disappeared when she added that she'd had a crush on a lot of boys in high school!

Six months after that fateful night, we were engaged, and six months after that, we were married.

Thirteen months later, My Beloved wife gave birth to the first of our two biological children, both boys. Then we adopted a two-month-old girl from Chile.

We've come a long way from those kids playing hide-and-seek in the dark.

And along the way, we've made our dreams come true.

About the Author

Russ Towne lives with his wife in Campbell, California. They've been married since 1979. They have three adult children, four grandsons, and a granddaughter on the way. In addition to enjoying his family and friends, and his dual passions for investing and writing, Russ loves to spend time in nature, especially near rivers and streams that run through giant redwood groves and near beautiful beaches. He loves reading, watching classic movies, and tending to his small fern garden and redwood grove. Russ manages the investments of the wealth management firm he founded in 2003.

Russ has written, compiled, and published two dozen books that can be found on Amazon.com.

You'll find his Amazon Author's Page at www.amazon.com/author/russtowne.

The titles of the books he has written, compiled, published, and released include:

Nonfiction

Reflections from the Heart of a Grateful Man

From the Heart of a Grateful Man

Reflections of a Grateful Man

Slices of Life—An anthology
of the selected nonfiction stories of several writers

Stop Peeing in the Kitty Litter

Fiction

Touched—Short stories and flash fiction

Palpable Imaginings—An anthology of fictional short stories
by several writers in various genres.

Poetry

Kaleidoscope
Tickletoe Tree Poetry—Humorous rhyming story poems for
children and those who are young at heart

Heart Whispers—An anthology of the selected works
of over twenty poets

Books for Young Children

The Beach That Love Built
Tickletoe Tree Poetry
A Day in the Shade of a Tickletoe Tree
The Grumpadinkles
Zach and the Toad Who Rode a Bull
Misty Zebracorn
V. G. and Dexter Dufflebee
Ki-Gra's REALLY, REALLY BIG Day!
The Duck Who Flew Upside Down
Clyde and Friends
Clyde and Hoozy Whatzadingle
Clyde and I Help a Hippo to Fly
Rusty Bear and Thomas Too
Clyde and I

Blogs

A Grateful Man (nonfiction uplifting posts): RussTowne.com

A Grateful Man's Poetry: AGratefulMansPoetry.com

Imaginings of a Grateful Man (fictional short stories): ImaginingsofaGratefulMan.com

Clyde and Friends (about writing children's stories): ClydeandFriends.com

Russ hopes readers experience truth and kindness in his writing, to remind everyone of the greatness and goodness within themselves and others.

www.ingramcontent.com/pod-product-compliance
Lightning Source LLC
Chambersburg PA
CBHW070639150426
42811CB00050B/401